Now I've Got You!

"Coloured Bedtime StoryBook"

By

Manohar Chamoli

Illustrated by

Mayukh Gosh

ILLUSTRATED & PUBLISHED
BY
E-KİTAP PROJESİ & CHEAPEST BOOKS

www.cheapestboooks.com

 www.facebook.com/EKitapProjesi

ISBN: 978-625-6308-69-5

Copyright, 2024 by e-Kitap Projesi
Istanbul

Categories: Adventure, Community
Country of Origin: United States
Cover: © Cheapest Books
License: CC-BY-4.0

For full terms of use and attribution, http://creativecommons.org/licenses/by/4.0/

Contributing: Hira Maharjan

© All rights reserved.

Except for the conditions stated in the License, no part of this book shall be reproduced or transmitted in any form or by any means, electronic or mechanical, including photocopy, recording or by any information or retrieval system, without written permission form the publisher.

About the Book

One day, Frog catches Wasp. "Now I've got you!" Frog says. But Wasp sees that Frog is in trouble, too! In a humorous chain of events, each animal is caught and nearly eaten by another, until Wasp comes up with a clever solution to save them all!

"Now I've got you!" said the Frog.

"Too bad for you!" said the Wasp.

"Why?" asked Frog.

"Look behind you," said the Wasp.

"Now I've got you!" said the Snake.

"Too bad for you," said the Frog.

"Why?" asked the Snake.

"Look behind you," said the Frog.

"Now I've got you!" said the Mongoose.

"Too bad for you," said the Snake.

"Why?" asked the Mongoose.

"Look behind you," said the Mongoose.

"Now I've got you!" said the Eagle.

"Frog, let me go and I will save us all!" yelled the wasp.

The Frog let go of the wasp.

The wasp flew up and stung the Eagle hard on her neck.

The Eagle let go of the Mongoose.

The Mongoose let go of the Snake.

The Snake let go of the Frog.

KER-SPLASH!

Everyone said, "Thank you, Wasp!"

And the Alligator thought, "Now I've got you..."

End of the Story

www.ingramcontent.com/pod-product-compliance
Lightning Source LLC
LaVergne TN
LVHW070454080526
838202LV00035B/2832